Gift to:
_____

From:
_____

Date:
_____

Whispers from Children's Hearts

An inspirational look into the minds and hearts of children around the world

RISA PUBLICATIONS

This book is dedicated to the children of the world

For my parents Anya Thompson and Harry Haisha

WHISPERS
from
Children's Hearts

Written by Lisa Haisha   Illustrated by Tim Huhn

Copyright © 2006

Written by Lisa Haisha   Artwork and Design by Tim Huhn

All rights reserved. This book may not be reproduced, in whole or in part, in any form or by any means electronic or mechanical, including photocopying, recording, or by any information storage or retrieval system now known or hereafter invented, with the permission from the publisher, Risa Publications.

Risa Publications
8424-A Santa Monica Blvd.
Suite 175
West Hollywood, CA 90069

www.whispersfromchildrenshearts.com

Library of Congress Cataloging-in-Publication data

Contents

Australia 8
China 12
France 16
Iraq 20
Israel 24
Italy 28
Japan 32
Macau 36
Malaysia 40
Mexico 44
Nepal 48
Netherlands 52
Peru 56
Singapore 60
United States 64

*"There are not seven wonders of the world in the eyes of a child.
There are seven million."*

-Walt Streightiff

"There are not seven wonders of the world in the eyes of a child.
There are seven million."

-Walt Streightiff

Introduction

Whisper's from Children's Hearts is more than a collection of children's quotes; it is a journey into the hearts and minds of conscious and concerned children around the globe. I have sat, knelt, or squatted to meet these youthful denizens eye to eye, heart to heart, in hopes of gaining insight into their thoughts and feelings and thus a better sense of their country.

In the course of my conversations, I asked each child the same three thought-provoking questions:

If you had one wish what would it be?

Is God fair? Why or why not?

Who in the world would you most want to meet?

Cradled in the following pages are the priceless answers to these questions. I spoke to more than 250 sometimes wise, sometimes whimsical, but always honest children of ages four through nine from Australia, China, France, Iraq, Israel, Italy, Japan, Macau, Malaysia, Nepal, Netherlands, Peru, Singapore, and the United States. Their responses were as varied as their cultures.

In the Middle East, few of these children had ever met an American; they were leery at first and very shy. It took several hours of sitting with them before they finally opened up, but once they did they shared their passions freely.

One girl from an Iraq orphanage told me she loved dogs; another wanted to be an artist and shared with me sketches of her friends.

Simply speaking with these children healed personal wounds and built bridges. One little Iraqi boy asked me why I was being so nice to them. Another shy boy who had never opened up wanted to know why I was "pretending to be nice," angrily stating that he knew after I left I would bomb them. This reality made me feel awful. I looked into their sad eyes as I told them I loved them and would never forget them. I let them know that most Americans did not want to hurt them; many wanted to help. Some were shocked and could not believe it, others cried in relief, feeling safer. My asking these three simple questions had truly become a way of connecting and mending hearts.

In Europe, I was surprised at how free-spirited and adult-like the children were. Many spoke several languages and had a great sense of fashion and art. They seemed intelligent and alive. They had many hopes and dreams and often idolized American celebrities and their life styles.

In Asia, most of the children acted shy, hiding behind their mother's skirts. But they flirted with me, inevitably peeking out and flashing a big smile. Most Asian children are taught not to talk with strangers, and parents are very protective - especially in China where for many years only one child per couple was allowed. But after bribing some of these parents with gifts of pencils, blue jeans, and T-shirts from Hollywood, they became more accommodating. And I discovered that their children really did want to talk, and had a lot to say.

To the adult ear, some quotes may seem a bit too honest, or too political, or too religious in tone to have been uttered by young children. Yet, they have not been altered in any fashion. Most young children have not yet learned to turn away from the single face of truth; they speak it blatantly, often displaying a wisdom not always found in their elders.

I wanted to include all the voices I heard, not just the simplistic and innocent ones. Some of these children live in countries where they are denied the basic human right of free speech, and while all children deserve to be heard I felt those denied a voice in their own countries deserved special consideration in this collection.

In each city I visited, I met children at schools, orphanages, and hospitals, as well as in common areas such as restaurants, parks, and on the street. Some parents wondered why I wanted to ask their children questions. I explained that through the children's eyes I garnered a purer sense of their countries. Trusting my intent, most of the adults I approached were amenable. I did, however, meet a few parents who declined permission, and I respected their wishes.

When I first began this project, my intention was to simply enjoy the company of children around the world. But later, in reading back through all the quotes I gathered in my travels, I realized I had collected far more than charming children's thoughts. My journals revealed the profound power of purpose, truth, and hope embedded in the soul of each child. Children have the ability to show us things we can't always see ourselves, to tell us the truths we don't always want to hear, and to remind us of that which we have forgotten. They reflect our adult world in its purest form, and we would do well to heed what they tell us.

To honor their parents' requests, and out of respect for their privacy and safety, I have not used any child's last name. Individual identities are not important in any case, for the children in this book represent children everywhere. I simply give you their hearts.

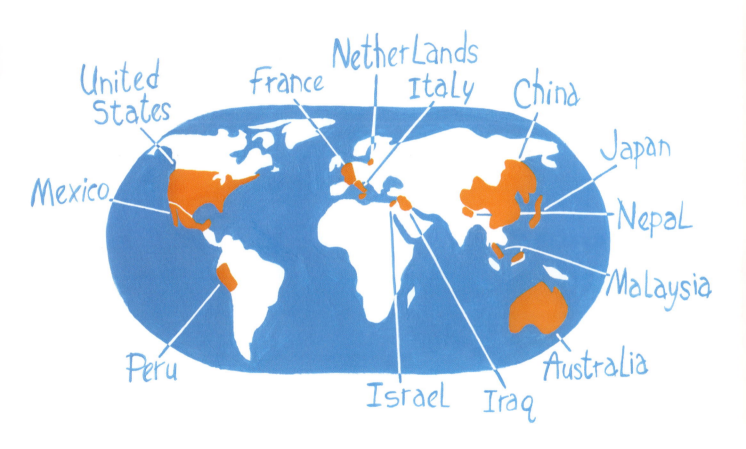

🇦🇺 Australia 🇦🇺

Who in the world would you most want to meet?

My angels that watch over me because I'd want to ask them why they chose me to protect. And I'm curious if one of them is my father who died.
- Patrick (8)

Australia

If you had one wish what would it be?

I'd make a wave big enough so I could surf all the way to Africa and not have to go to school.
 - Caleb (7)

I would make all kids beautiful so nobody would get picked on, not even my friend Robin.
 - Emma (8)

I'd make adults nicer because then kids at school would be nicer and wouldn't want to hurt other kids.
 I don't think adults know this.
 - Evan (8)

My wish would be to be able to make a real baby instead of having pretend ones.
 - Hilary (5)

I would ice skate in the Olympics, and have everyone look at me the whole time. I'd win for my mommy too.
 - Olivia (5)

Australia

Is God fair? Why or why not?

Yes, God is fair because he protects us every day and he never asks for any favor in return.
— Conner (6)

Yes, because he helped my brother heal when we asked him to.
— Angela (6)

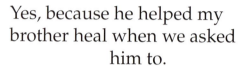

I don't think he's fair because some people are mean and selfish, especially at my school. But maybe they work for God and are supposed to be that way to teach us something. I don't know.
— *Jason (9)*

Yes because I talk to him every night and he listens to me even when my parents don't.
— Nicole (8)

Yes, because my favorite teacher at school loves him and she's honest.
— Giles (8)

Australia

Who in the world would you most want to meet?

My sister Jessie because I never thought she'd die so young. I never got to tell her things like how nice she was to me. She taught me how to write my name.
- Olivia (8)

Jesus, God, Buddha, Mohammad and Allah. I'd want to know why they love everyone and the people who follow their way don't.
- Spencer (7)

I'd like to meet myself after I die so I would have evidence of life after death. Then if it were true, I'd be a better person. If not, I'm gonna goof off.
Derek (6)

Picasso. I would like to paint like him. And he had so many friends and women who wanted him to paint them. That would be cool.
- John (9)

China

If you had one wish what would it be?

My wish would be to dance forever and to have red hair.
- Jiang (7)

China

If you had one wish what would it be?

I would make my mommy well by holding her hand because she likes that. It makes her smile.
— Wu (6)

I wish that I could have helped build the world and create the animals because I wouldn't have made them scared of us or enjoy eating us. Then even the tigers wouldn't want to bite me. I'd love to play with them.
— Liu (8)

I would wish that I could travel the world and make friends in all the countries and learn everything and then have China make a big party for the world and make peace with my new friends everywhere.
— Zhang (9)

I would wish that I had lots of brothers and sisters because I get so lonely playing by myself when my parents are working. But my parents work because they love me so much.
— Jin (6)

China

Is God Fair? Why or why not?

No I don't believe in God but I believe in Buddha. He is the man that changed people's thinking forever.
 - Lee (9)

Yes, because we have life. I believe God is more powerful than just a name. He is everything we touch, breathe, and think.
 - Shen (7)

No, because we are here alone but there are special teachers guiding us.
 - Kistan (9)

There is no God but there is something special out there that makes the planet live but it's not just one person. I think it is a bunch of people.
 - Lian (8)

No, because there is no God. People who believe in him are silly. We are here to suffer, then die. Then we can be happy.
 - Hinda (9)

China

Who in the world would you most want to meet?

I would like to meet the person who will save the world from fighting and bring peace and love into peoples hearts.
My mommy said that person will be coming soon. But she doesn't know his name.
- Fujji (7)

My cousin Kwang because he protected me when he lived here. Now he moved far away to Xian.
- Angelina (4)

Buddha because I think we need him here to help us have peace.
- Kwang (6)

France

If you had one wish what would it be?

I would make people be nice because the waiter in the restaurant wouldn't even cook my bacon. When I asked him to, he got real mad and yelled at me. My mommy said we should be nice to waiters who are not nice because they need love the most.

- Pierre (7)

France

If you had one wish what would it be?

I wish that I could be
   as cheerful as the sun.
I know the sun gets
   sad sometimes because
he doesn't show up
   some days but he does
     most of the time.
       - Monique (9)

My wish would be to be more like my brother because he is so smart and everyone gives him all the attention. My mommy said once that I wasn't as special as him and that made me cry. But, I know I am because my aunt said we're all special in our own way and she is smart.
       - Cody (5)

I would become the
   richest person in the
world because rich
   people are always
      laughing.
      - Giselle (7)

I would wish that I could go to doggie heaven and look for Perrier who was hit by a car last month and died.
       - Isabel (7)

France

Is God fair? Why or why not?

I'm not sure because my mommy said God is not alive but she might be wrong because my friend Simone said she saw him once.
— Pauline (8)

Yes, he's fair because we talk about him in school and my teacher says that he makes the right decisions even if we don't understand them.
— Carl (7)

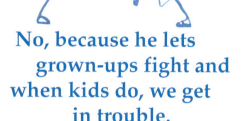

No, because he lets grown-ups fight and when kids do, we get in trouble.
— Oliver (7)

Yes, because everyone tells him to leave us alone and nobody cares about what he says so now everyone is unhappy.
— Ginette (6)

Yes, because everyone knows that God is fair but I don't think he's been that nice to me lately but I will try harder to be good.
— Marguerite (6)

France

Who in the world would you most want to meet?

Mickey Mouse because he is silly and fun.
— Christina (5)

The Queen of England because I believe I should marry Prince William and become royalty because I would like that.
— Charlotte (8)

I'd like to meet Paris in the twenties because it was full of art and passion. I love to paint and want to work with Picasso or someone happy like him.
— Paul (9)

Your President because I want to know how to make money like Americans. Then I would copy him and make us rich.
— Michelle (7)

Iraq

If you had one wish what would it be?

I would send hugs and kisses to my sister in the United States and make sure she's happy because she has no family there except for her husband and when we talk on the phone we are always crying because we miss each other so much.
- Inari (7)

Iraq

If you had one wish what would it be?

I would give everyone a nice home to live in that doesn't leak, and food to eat because my dad says we live like animals because of all the conflict in the world.
    That isn't normal.
      - Jamal (7)

That God will let me live long enough to see things that will make me cry out of happiness instead of sadness.
    - Ramzi (5)

My wish would be to tell your president that his bombs really hurt us.
  Maybe he doesn't know.
    - Laith (9)

My wish would be to feed my family everyday, even the days we get bombed.
    - Efraim (8)

Iraq

Is God Fair? Why or why not?

Yes, because we have suffering. My mommy cries everyday because my brother is missing and she thinks he might be dead.

So God must think we're strong enough to handle the pain.
— Malik (8)

Yes, because war has been part of my whole life and it has made me strong.

It is all I dream about. I dream about being in Heaven with my family and lots of people there with us, laughing, just like we're all from the same country.
— Azawi (9)

No, because nobody likes our country and wants to hurt us and I don't know why. Is that fair?
— Adem (9)

No, we believe in Mohammad. If there was someone higher than him, like a God then our country wouldn't be so poor. And people would care about us instead of being friends with money.
— Akil (7)

Yes, because life is just a test then we get to live on forever and eat good food and play all day if we pass.
— Mansur (6)

Iraq

Who in the world would you most want to meet?

I'd want to meet God to understand my purpose and why I'm here.
I just don't understand the reason for life.
My mommy says there is no reason. Just live because you were born.

— Kamal (8)

The American president because I'd like to let him know how nice we are.
I think if he met me he would like me. And then protect my family because he likes to have fun. I've seen him on TV smiling a lot and my family is fun.

— Zia (9)

I'd meet your president to ask him why he lets his bombs fall on my daddy. And I'd want to ask an American doctor to bring medicine. Because we don't have any left and we're sick.

— Walid (7)

 Israel

Who in the world would you most want to meet?

Jesus, so I can ask him to save us again because we lost our way.
- Judith (4)

Israel

If you had one wish what would it be?

I'd have peace in the whole world.

My wish would be to take all the money and build my family a hundred palaces and play in them all day.
— Zachary (8)

I'd want everyone to like each other so people in my family don't have to die anymore just because of our religion.
— Gabe (7)

I wish that I could have all the money in the world so me and my family could feel safe.
— Mikkel (8)

I would collect all the bombs in the world and destroy them one by one so we could all live in peace. I'd get the Nobel Peace Prize.
— Adam (9)

Israel

Is God Fair? Why or why not?

Yes, because he gave us Israel.
                          - Aaron (8)

Yes, because he said we were the chosen ones and he helps us to stay safe.
                          - Gabe (9)

Yes, because Jesus was here talking about him a lot. And people saw him die and then be alive again.
                          - Adam (7)

Yes, because he lived here. I've seen Bethlehem.
                          - Mikkel (9)

Israel

Who in the world would you most want to meet?

My mommy who died when I was born because I miss her hugs when I'm sad.
- Amira (5)

Sylvester Stallone because I want to be like him. Because nobody would pick on him because he is strong and in control.
- Ariel (8)

Jesus because I want to ask him why he took my daddy from me. I'm only seven. He must have a reason but I'd like him back.
- Yithak (7)

God, so he can tell everyone to leave us alone. Because my father was killed and my uncle doesn't have a leg.
- Reharam (8)

Italy

If you had one wish what would it be?

I would sing all day long, so I could perform for the world and my parents would be very proud.
- Aria (6)

Italy

If you had one wish what would it be?

I wish that I could make my mommy work less because she works so much.

But I miss her and think she should have my love instead of thinking about money.

— Maria (7)

I would make lots of money and buy a big house and move my mommy in on one side and my daddy on the other because then they might kiss again.

— Vito (5)

I wish I could meet Madonna and that she would teach me how to act because she is so talented at it and makes everyone watch her.

— Lucia (8)

Italy

Is God Fair? Why or why not?

Yes, because I talk to him every day with my mommy and daddy before we eat.
    - Giovanni (9)

Yes, because we go to church and it's peaceful and smells nice .
I bet God smells nice, too.
    -Vito (7)

Yes, because
he does what
he thinks is
right
even if we
think he is a
bad manager.
    - Carlo (8)

Yes, because my mommy thinks so but I'm not sure because I've never met him so he's hard to understand sometimes.
    - Pasquale (6)

Italy

Who in the world would you most want to meet?

People in the land of fairy tales and dreams because I can learn from them because they are always pretending and nothing is real.
— Beatrice (7)

Fellini because he makes fantasy films. My dad watches his movies and lets me watch, too.
— Geseppe (8)

Mussolini because my teacher talks about him a lot and I would want people to still talk about me when I'm dead.
— Antonio (9)

The pope because he could heal mommy with his connections to God because God trusts him.
— Antoinette (8)

Japan

Who in the world would you most want to meet?

All the sumo wrestlers because they look funny and they make a lot of money for playing. I'd want to make money playing too.
- Nakamura (6)

Japan

If you had one wish what would it be?

I'd never go to school again because my brain hurts from having to think so much.

- Hoshi (9)

I would become the first woman president in Japan, like Hilary Clinton.
-- Suki (9)

I'd want to marry Cleopatra and rub her tummy and massage her feet every night before she goes to sleep.

- Taka (8)

I'd want to go camping everyday to cook rice with my father because then maybe he wouldn't want to work so much.

- Kyoshi (7)

Japan

Is God Fair? Why or why not?

Yes, because if everyone is
equal, there is no boss.
Thats life.
Even bees...
some are weak and some are strong.
- Hirohito (7)

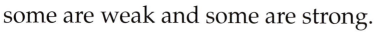

*God does not exist;
otherwise, he would give
everyone the same
opportunity.
But buddha exists.*
- Miyoko (8)

Yes, she's fair, sneaky but fair.

- Keiko (6)

*Yes, he needs variety.
So there are good people and
bad people like on TV.*
- Takeo (9)

Without God people cannot mentally
be safe. They have to think they'll go
to Heaven.
That means God exists for everybody.
- Zenzo (9)

Japan

Who in the world would you most want to meet?

Audrey Hepburn because my mommy loves her and said God blessed her more than other people.
- Yuki (5)

Your president because he's smart and rules the world. I'd like to do that some day.
- Takashi (8)

The man on the moon because I'd like to visit the moon with my mommy and I'd want to ask him what to bring.
- Roko (9)

Macau

If you had one wish what would it be?

My wish would be to climb the tallest mountain in the world until I reached the sky and could touch the clouds and play with the stars.
- Kaniel (5)

Macau

If you had one wish what would it be?

I'd make my brother alive again.
       - Kersan (6)

I would move to America so we could make lots of money and live at Disneyland.
       - Lalasa (7)

I would have my mom cook warm food for everyone who came to our restaurant even if they couldn't pay.
       -Minnie (8)

My wish would be to become rich so I could help my daddy pay for us because he works three jobs and is always tired.
       - Shin (8)

Macau

Is God Fair? Why or why not?

I think we are God. Every thing is up to us. We can choose to be happy or we can choose to be sad.

We are very poor but my daddy and mommy make us happy.

— Fei (7)

Yes, because when I look up into the sky I can feel the warmth and safety of the stars and moon.

I can feel God watching over my family and me.

I think I have even spotted him once but he disappeared quickly.

— Lo (8)

I don't know because my dad is always so sad and doesn't talk to us very much because he works so hard.

Why would God make him work so hard?

Other dads don't work so hard.

— Chip (7)

Yes, because I know when I pray he can hear me even if he doesn't obey when I beg to him.

— Xujun (5)

Yes, because we are breathing. He made us and gave us so much and we always look at what he didn't give us.

— Shiu (8)

Macau

Who in the world would you most want to meet?

Buddha, because he helps me when I ask for advice. I not sure how he puts it there.

— Xinhua (8)

My daddy because he died and I don't remember him.
I only have one picture and this necklace (He showed me his leather necklace around his neck).

— Chang (6)

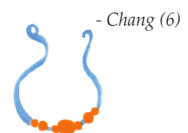

I would like to meet everyone at some point because I like meeting people. People are nice.

— Peng (7)

Malaysia

If you had one wish what would it be?

My wish is to make everyone happy and peaceful wearing smiles on their faces.
- Kamal (7)

Malaysia

If you had one wish what would it be?

I would become a really smart doctor because my mommy has cancer and is going to leave us soon because her doctor ran out of hope.
But I have some that I can give to him.

— Urinda (8)

My wish would be to get more sleep…at least ten hours a day because I haven't slept very much in months because I am helping my dad fix his store because it started falling apart.

— Matai (9)

I'd wish for all the money in the world to go to my daddy so he could help us and all our neighbors buy fun toys and food.

— Ramya (8)

I'd wish for everybody to be happy…no poor countries….everybody like a family.

— Rani (8)

Malaysia

Is God Fair? Why or why not?

No, because God should feed us and I'm always hungry and I'm told that I should be grateful for just being alive. That's strange isn't it?
— Tan (8)

Yes, because I don't have a mommy because she gave her life for me to be born.
So, God thought I didn't need a mommy. He believes I'm strong. I will do my best to help daddy.
— Irianto (7)

Yes, because he's God even though he's invisible. And life is life, whether it's good or bad.
— Ainon (8)

Yes, I guess because my mommy says so, but he doesn't seem fair all the time.
— Wang (8)

No, because my mommy and daddy always fight and God wouldn't put up with that. The ten commandments say we should all love thy neighbor.
— Hari (8)

Malaysia

Who in the world would you most want to meet?

I'd want to meet Donald Duck. He is my favorite person because he's so funny.
— Mohamad (7)

I don't know. Allah, because I want to know why he needs so much attention. Because we always have to be bowing to him and I get bored.
— Ramya (7)

Lee Kuen (ex-prime minister of Singapore) because my dad said he made Singapore happy and I would like to be like that.
— Alisa (6)

Lee Kuen because he was smart and we need help so we can play and mommy doesn't have to hit us.
— Kaniel (6)

 Mexico

If you had one wish what would it be?

I would help build houses for all the poor kids and families.
- Javier (7)

Mexico

If you had one wish what would it be?

My wish would be to live in America and take my mommy, daddy, and uncle with me because then we could live in a house that doesn't rain.

- Salina (6)

My wish would be to help my daddy understand that when he hurts my mommy that it is wrong and it makes everyone sad, even him.

- Hector (5)

My wish would be to quit school so I could get a job to help my family.

- Miguel (8)

My wish would be to go to school and learn all about the world so I could speak many languages and then become a doctor and heal people.

- Silvia (8)

Mexico

Is God Fair? Why or why not?

Yes, because he knows everything my mommy said because she is always apologizing to him.
— Beatriz (5)

No, because nothing is fair so why should God be fair.
— Jorge (7)

No, because we don't have a home.
But maybe he thinks my family doesn't need a home because he gave us warm weather.
I don't know.
It's confusing.
— Juanita (8)

Yes, God is fair because life is a struggle, like a test; if we pass and survive it, he will be nice later.
— Alberto (9)

Mexico

Who in the world would you most want to meet?

> Jesus. I have questions about how he died.
> — Fernando (7)

> Mother Theresa because I want her to bless my mommy because she's dying and nobody can help her.
> — Rosa (8)

> My daddy because he died a long time ago and my mommy said he was nice.
> — Carlos (6)

> Your president because I wrote him a letter and he didn't write back.
> — Flaca (9)

Nepal

Who in the world would you most want to meet?

I'd love to meet my grandmother because she was the first person to hold me and kiss my cheek.
- Genesa (5)

Nepal

If you had one wish what would it be?

My wish would be to make the people in Italy nice because this Italian boy tried to cut in line when we were at a movie and that is not nice.

— Beatrice (9)

I would make everyone happy by giving them a place to live and feeding them chicken and coca-cola.

— Ajay (9)

My wish would be to have magic powers and have everyone come to me for help because I would always help them.

They could trust me.

— Pandita (7)

Nepal

Is God Fair? Why or why not?

Yes, because my family is so nice. And my parents said that God lives inside each of us.
— Indra (7)

Yes, because I got to go to America with my daddy and I saw how God loves Americans because they have everything.
— Zaheer (9)

No, because I cry all day long because I don't trust anyone anymore because nobody gives my daddy work because he is sick and they don't want to get sick.

So he is always angry. And my mommy doesn't have food to cook.
— Sharad (8)

No, because my sister died because we couldn't get her to a doctor in time because he lives so far away and we had to walk.
— Anupam (7)

Nepal

Who in the world would you most want to meet?

The American president, to ask for his help because we need money and jobs.
- Vipul (9)

Mother Theresa because she could teach me how to help people because she can't do that anymore since she died. She was nice to sick people. My mommy thinks she was good.
- Pirna (7)

(Satya) Sai Baba because he could help my family by praying for us because he is so powerful because he is God's best friend.
- Rafik (6)

Netherlands

If you had one wish what would it be?

I wish I could talk to dragons and ride them around the world waving to everyone and dropping chocolates as I soar up, up, and away like Santa Claus.
- Roel (9)

Netherlands

If you had one wish what would it be?

I would wish that I could become my cat, Fluffy, because he comes and goes all day and my mom pets him all night. He has a good life.
- Yons (8)

I wish there was a park for all kids to have fun where they don't have to pay money because parks in Amsterdam cost too much so I can't play with my friends very often.
- Nigel (6)

I would make my imaginary life reality because there I am popular and exciting and everyone loves me.
- Zuza (7)

That my grandma would tell me stories again while we're outside watching the stars in the sky twinkle above because it makes me feel safe.
I love my grandma but she is getting sicker each day.
- Deman (7)

Netherlands

Is God Fair? Why or why not?

No, because me and my friends are bad sometimes and my mom says that if I am bad God will punish me and my friends and I haven't been punished yet so I think adults use God to scare kids.

— Peter (7)

Yes, because he is kind. He never tells on anybody and he sees everything.
— Elisabeth (6)

Yes, because he is always nice and patient because I don't see him punishing the mean kids.
— Pavel (8)

No, because God lets people lie. And he made us like him, in his image, so…
— Victor (7)

Netherlands

Who in the world would you most want to meet?

Anyone that is nice because
I like to have fun.
- Kaatje (6)

Anne Frank because she was Jewish and smart and so am I.
- Reka (5)

Madonna because she floats on stage and is magical.
- Nigel (9)

Hilary Clinton because she is clever.
My mommy told me she will be president soon.
- Rasine (9)

 Peru

If you had one wish what would it be?

I would want a new backpack because mine is ripped and things fall out.
- Abel (8)

Peru

If you had one wish what would it be?

I would learn how to cook because people here make bad food.
—Rosa Maria (7)

That I was older so I could find out things that kids don't know.
—Michael (12)

I would like people to remember me when they meet me.
—Yessenia (9)

To visit all the people who visit our country so I can see how they live too.
—Edith (10)

I want to become a teacher.
I want a bandana.
And to pray every day.
—Ruth (10)

My wish would be to fly in a plane really high.
—Sandro (6)

Peru

Is God Fair? Why or why not?

*Yes, God is fair because he made me
even though he knew it wouldn't be easy.
So, since making us was hard,
   we have it hard too so we can be the same.*

- Michael (12)

Yes, because I am deaf but so are all my friends.

- Ruth (10)

Yes, because we are where we are supposed to be.

- Felician (10)

I honor God and respect him because people hurt his son until he spilled blood. So everyone is the same so he's fair.

- Yessenia (9)

Life is fair even with Americans walking around with money and nice clothes.

- Marina (7)

Peru

Who in the world would you most want to meet?

New friends because I love hearing their stories.
— Edith (10)

People who have cameras because I like them to take my picture and show it to me. It's like magic.
— Ruth (10)

*God.
Because I want to change my plans here.
I want to start over.*
— Ricardo (9)

Jesus because we talk all the time even though we have never met.
— Samuel (9)

Jesus because he died for me and I think that was nice.
— Rosa Maria (7)

Anyone famous on TV so I can see if they look the same.
— Elvis (9)

Singapore

If you had one wish what would it be?

I would build a playground full of magical animals and ride the elephants and play hide and seek with the monkeys.
- Lee (9)

Singapore

If you had one wish what would it be?

My wish would be to walk around the world and say hello to everyone,
even if they looked different from me.
— Saul (8)

I would clean the world of pollution because we are clean and it's nice.
— Ching (7)

I would let Keiko move in with us and make her my sister.
— Hou (7)

Singapore

Is God Fair? Why or why not?

No, because we were created from the ocean and if there was a God he would have planned things differently.
— Farah (6)

Yes, because I love everyone and God made us like him and told us that love is the most important thing to strive for.
— Choo (8)

Yes, because peace is inside us all, if we look for it.
— Zi (8)

No, because we created ourselves and take care of ourselves. If God existed he could have visited us by now. My parents say they have never seen him.
— Aaryanna (7)

Singapore

Who in the world would you most want to meet?

Someone that would like to take me to fun places like Sentosa (*Singapore's large amusement park*), so I can play with the fireflies and dolphins.
— Leng (8)

The people I meet because I like them and I like the surprise of meeting new ones at school.
— Qiao (7)

Lee Kuen (Ex-Prime Minister of Singapore) because he's number one in Asia because he made us go from poor to rich and now many people visit us.
— Zhu (9)

United States

Who in the world would you most want to meet?

The first human to walk the earth, and I'd ask them what it felt like, what they saw.
- Cory (8)

United States

If you had one wish what would it be?

My wish would be that you buy me a Barbie doll.
— Emi (4)

I would move to Paris and let my parents visit me once a week.
— Daniella (5)

I would live in a big castle and give orders to everybody. Then laugh with them.
— Cheryl (9)

I would put money in everyone's birthday card so when they opened it they can be happy. Kids like money.
— Tom (7)

United States

Is God Fair? Why or why not?

Yes, 'cause he gave every single one of us friendship and some of us don't have it anymore 'cause they forgot about it or left it somewhere.
- Jordan (5)

Yes, because God lives in the coolest place where everyone wants to live. And God is inside everyone so he has to be fair or he hurts himself.
- Carli (5)

No, because some bad kids get mad and keep it inside them and then get guns and hurt other kids because they're so sad.
But the happy kids can't protect themselves and get hurt.
- Parker (9)

Yes, because he's always watching and protecting us.
- Annette (7)

Yes, because my teachers make us say prayers to him every morning in school. If he wasn't fair, that would be silly.
- Myles (6)

United States

Who in the world would you most want to meet?

Martin Luther King. He put the whites and the blacks together.
He was a really great person.
- Camille (6)

My great grandpa. He died before I was born. I feel sorry for him because he didn't get to meet me after I was old.
But he said,
"good luck"
to me before he died.
- Patty (5)

People I can't meet now...

like George Washington or someone that was related to me.
- John (8)

Contact us

For more information about
Whispers from Children's Hearts
Please visit our website:
www.whispersfromchildrenshearts.com

featuring photos from Lisa'a trips, upcoming books, products

Special Thanks to:

Lee Aronsohn for your belief in me and this book. You are also one of my greatest inspirations. This book would not exist without your love and support. And thank you for sharing with me your tremendous heart and soul, I feel knowing you has been a privilege and has altered my life for the better. **Randell McCormick** for your hard work and dedication not only on this book but all my projects and ideas. Without your creativity and love this book would not have reached the magical level I feel it has captured. You are truely my best friend, my family and one of the most incredible human beings alive. **Tim Huhn** for sharing your artistic talents on this book and being so awsome to work with. **Maria Belknap** for your incredible editing skills and creativity, and love. **David Bergeaud** for always believing in me and starting me off on my creative path and constantly inspiring me to do more. **Valerio DeGuevara** for helping me nurture and discover this book and believing that the children's voices were important to share with the world. **John Gomez** for your hard work and talent in designing a demo for us. **Alix Haisha**, my twin sister, for contributing many creative ideas and time into this project. Your talent and love for children contributed greatly, helping make this book be the best it could be. **Deborah Kagen** for being there for me as my confidante, shrink, and best friend for the past decade. **Carsten Lorenz** for your free spirit and insatible appetite for life. It's contagious. **Ashley Mammo** for your incredible energy, curiosity, love, and partner in crime. You have been with me through many of my journeys and they wouldn't have been the same without you. **Dan Millman** for your encouragement and belief in the project in it's rawest stage and encouraging me to dig deeper. **Fred Powers** for helping me discover the title of this book and for being the rock in my life for the past 15 years. Your creativity, passion for life, and strength have inspired me forever. **Michael Ran** for all your support. I appreciate you for generously sharing your talent and creativity. **June Saruwatari** for your incredible organizational skills that helped me stay on track and on purpose. **Sassan Saatchi** for being a magical loving being that is always inspiring. **Scott Smith** for your wisdom and artistic contributions, which were immeasurable. **Gayana Revelle** and **Gary Ulmer** for going on the journey with me. I feel blessed to have you both in my life. And **Ben Vereen** for your incredible spirit and deep faith that you spread throughout the world. It has been an honor to work closely with you.

Much love and thanks to: Karen Asaro, Tom Brennan, John Campbell, Luis Colina, Diane DeForest, Peter Dekom, John Denos, Candice Doi, Mark Gambol, Rick Gibbs, Gary Gibson, Julie Haisha, Steve Hardison, Lesa Hardy, Flor Katz, Sandra and Karl Larson, Michael Levine, Bill Meyers, Patrick Michael, Theresa Moujaes, Joe Ochman, Terra Ryan, Glenda Shaw, Don Smith, Brad Sorensen, Kevin Thranow, Baek Sik Wang, Julia Wyson, Tatsuo Yakota.